Christmas at Home with Rita MacNeil

Christmas at Home

with

Rita MacNeil

KEY PORTER  BOOKS

National Library of Canada Cataloguing in Publication Data

MacNeil, Rita, 1944–
    Christmas at home with Rita MacNeil

ISBN 1-55263-476-0

    1. MacNeil, Rita, 1944– 2. Christmas—Anecdotes. 3. Christmas cookery. 4. Christmas decorations. 5. Christmas music. I. Title.

ML420.M169A3 2002   394.2663   C2002-903524-4

The Canada Council | Le Conseil des Arts
for the Arts | du Canada

ONTARIO ARTS COUNCIL
CONSEIL DES ARTS DE L'ONTARIO

The publisher gratefully acknowledges the support of the Canada Council for the Arts and the Ontario Arts Council for its publishing program.

We acknowledge the financial support of the Government of Canada through the Book Publishing Industry Development Program (BPIDP) for our publishing activities.

Key Porter Books Limited
70 The Esplanade
Toronto, Ontario
Canada M5E 1R2

www.keyporter.com

Cover design: Peter Maher
Electronic formatting and text design: Jack Steiner
Page 115 represents a continuation of this copyright page.

Printed and bound in Canada

03 04 05 06 07 08 6 5 4 3 2 1

Contents

O Tannenbaum!

I spent the early part of my childhood in Big Pond, Cape Breton, Nova Scotia. In later years, I lived thirty miles away in what is now the city of Sydney, and I lived in Toronto from 1962 until the late seventies. But my fondest memories are of Big Pond. I think the place where you grow up always holds a particular emotional power. Through my stories and music, I have talked of its beauty and shared with others my love for the place I call home.

To me, the village has always had an old-fashioned feel to it. Perhaps this is because when I was a child, my father told me stories about Big Pond and the way things were when he was a boy. As I listened, I could picture all the places he talked about and, really, not much had changed. His descriptions evoked images of people travelling by sleigh or horse and buggy, visiting neighbours and making merry, especially around Christmas. I remember a few folks who did use a horse and sleigh occasionally when I was young. Even now I can hear the sound of the sleigh bells, the creak of the leather harness, the squeal of the runners through the new packed

One of the many small ponds that lure skaters

How the Village Came to Be

Music and Lyrics by Rita MacNeil

I'd like to tell a story
My father told me
About our little village
And how it came to be

It was just before his birthday
There was not a tree in sight
There wasn't any water
Or little hills to climb

The land stretched out forever
With not a soul for miles
In fact the only thing to see
Was far up in the sky

For there were stars of every shape
All dancing in the night
The moon was moving through the clouds
Casting streams of light

Then something finally happened
That stood the test of time
A star shone out of nowhere
Bigger than them all

Golden dust fell on the land
And trees began to grow
Little hills kept popping up
And folks began to show

They gathered in a circle
And marvelled in delight
And just as they were smiling
A pond came into sight

The water soon reflected
The moon and stars above
This miracle of ages
Brought certain peace and love

And as they stood in silence
It soon came clear to all
This tiny little village
Would now become Big Pond

I know it's just a story
But when I was child
Our father told a lot of tales
That gave us many smiles

snow and the horses' snorts and whinnies as they inhaled the sharp cold air.

I can remember skaters on the ponds, their hand-knit scarves trailing out behind them as they sped around the glistening ice, and children on toboggans sliding down the gently sloping hills around the village. Snowfalls created a winter wonderland where children would play for hours, their cries of delight echoing throughout those all-too-short December afternoons.

I can picture as well the adults, particularly the men, gathering at the general store, where the warmth of the pot-bellied stove on a brisk winter day was a welcome attraction. Shaking the snow from their boots, they would enter the store, greet each other and extend

their cold-reddened hands toward the stove. Then, unbuttoning their heavy overcoats, one might take out his pipe, another would extract some chewing tobacco from a pouch, and the conversation would start to flow. They could spend hours exchanging local news and gossip, expounding on the latest political developments in Cape Breton or the world at large and, when all such topics were finally exhausted, simply talking about the weather. Every now and then they would glance out the window, remark on how the wind was rising or the snow was blowing, and inch closer to the stove that drew them in like a magnet.

Occasionally, a woman from the village might enter the store to purchase some small necessity, and then the men would respectfully pause in their discussions to greet her. The women didn't usually join in these rambling conversations around the stove. Even if it had been considered seemly for them to do so, at that time of year they would have had much too much to do at home, what with cleaning their houses from top to bottom and preparing the holiday fare, as they got ready for the Christmas season. Of course, when it came to baking, they would make everything from scratch and perform small miracles with whatever they could afford by way of ingredients.

That is how I have always pictured the village, and when I was growing up, it was still very much like that. A lot of the homes my father recalled from years gone by were still standing. The old farmhouses all had a certain charm about them. They were usually two storeys, with a staircase at the front of the house, while some had another one in the kitchen leading up to a back bedroom. This staircase would be used by the woman of the house when she came down to the kitchen early in the morning to start the fire in the stove

A typical village scene throughout Cape Breton

before anyone else got up. All the homes were made of wood. In my grandmother's house, there was a room called the "good room," which is where you would find lovely handmade doilies draped over the arms of the chesterfield and chairs, giving the room that old-world feeling. Outside, the peaks of the houses had a single window that always made us children wonder what or who was up there. But when we were little, visiting with our parents, we never got beyond the kitchen, for this was the focal point where everyone gathered.

There was always something magical about winter in Big Pond, the way the snow fell softly and settled on the vast fields and in dense woods, clinging to the branches of the green spruce and creating the perfect playground for every child who lived there. On the rooftops of all the houses in view, there was just the right amount of snow for Santa to land his sleigh and his eight reindeer.

That is the scene I gazed upon from my desk in our one-room schoolhouse, where the large windows allowed the students to view the magic of the approaching holiday season. We sat at our desks, supposedly concentrating on arithmetic and English composition, but daydreaming was unavoidable. Our eyes were wide open, filled with that excited look children get when they know Christmas is just around the corner. All the signs were there: adults exchanging smiles and us children talking endlessly about our Christmas wishes, what we hoped to get and how good we were going to be to make sure Santa would come.

At home, the old box of decorations would be hauled out from its place of storage, even though the custom was to wait to decorate

Delightful dolls, one of the many gifts I receive around Christmas

until Christmas Eve. Two weeks before the big day, Christmas cards began to arrive in the mail. As they were placed around the house, we would gaze at the vivid Christmas scenes, and our excitement would grow. We had so much to look forward to. Everything seemed larger than life as each day drew us closer to the big event. Gifts seemed to appear out of nowhere. I learned later that folks who could afford to bought their presents through the Eaton's catalogue or drove the thirty miles to Sydney to shop at a few department stores, like Stedman's or Crowell's, where credit was available.

On the morning of the second-last day of school, we would go out to the nearby woods to choose and cut down a Christmas tree for the classroom. With so many beautiful trees around our little school-house, there was always one—usually a spruce—that was big and heavy, with lush green branches. Once it was carried into the school-house, we put the tree in a corner and were all allowed to take part in the decorating.

Over the years, people had donated ornaments for the school tree, and we would dig them out of the box with great anticipation. Each year, the other pupils and I would greet each decoration with delight. Even though we saw the same little baubles every year, we'd more or less forget about them after the holidays, so it was like seeing them for the first time when they came out of the box. We'd spend the early part of the afternoon hanging the brightly coloured bells and balls and winding paper ribbon around each branch of the magnificent tree. We used red and green tissue paper to fill up any bare spots on our tree.

Even the youngest students got to proudly place trinkets among the great branches, and everyone felt part of something special. Many of the ornaments were made of glass, so accidents were unavoidable. But even the shattering sound of a coloured ball slipping from the hands of an overexcited child and crashing to the wooden floor was no cause for alarm. After all, it was the season to be jolly.

We were even allowed to talk out loud. Back then, for better or for worse, the rule in the classroom was silence unless you were called upon to speak by the teacher, so when that rule was relaxed, a deafening but happy racket arose as children chattered and joked.

Finally, it would be time to place the star—a large, silvery, five-pointed affair—on top of the tree. Our teacher, Mary, would carefully climb up on a chair and reach up to position the star on the topmost branch. Once the star was in place, our tree was complete. The smell of wet mittens drying by the big old stove in the centre of the room all but disappeared as the fragrant scent of spruce filled our nostrils.

On this day, we'd also put our names in a box, and draw to see whom we'd be giving a gift to. The children ranged from grade one to grade nine, and we always picked separately for our own age group. I always hoped I would pick a girl's name—it was easier to buy or make something a little girl would like. You could colour a pretty box, or buy a little plastic doll or bows or ribbons for braided hair.

An Angel Ornament

Materials

cloth • needle and thread • glue (a glue gun works best) • lace • thread or string • cotton for stuffing • ribbon • wire or pipe cleaner

Instructions

1. Draw two different-sized circles on the cloth and cut them out. The larger circle will make the body and the smaller will make the wings.

2. Sew or glue lace on the edge of each circle (hot glue from a glue gun will make this easier).

3. Put a little bit of cotton in the centre of the larger circle and use a piece of string or thread to tie the cloth around the cotton to make a head.

4. Tie string or thread in the middle of the small circle, making two pie-piece shapes for the wings. Attach the wings to the neck of the body with a thread or glue.

5. Tie ribbon in a bow around the neck.

6. Make a halo from wire or a pipe cleaner and glue it onto the top of the head.

7. Sew a loop of thread to the angel's back for hanging the ornament.

Tea, anyone?

Before we all went home for the day, we helped clean up, sprinkling Dustbane on the floor to be swept and wiping the chalkboard extra hard, leaving it almost like new. All this cleaning was in preparation for the next day, when our Christmas party

Away in a Manger

Traditional

Away in a manger, no crib for a bed,
The little Lord Jesus laid down his sweet head.
The stars in the bright sky looked down where He lay,
The little Lord Jesus asleep on the hay.

The cattle are lowing, the poor Baby wakes,
But little Lord Jesus no crying He makes.
I love thee, Lord Jesus, look down from the sky,
And stay by my cradle till morning is nigh.

Be near me Lord Jesus, I ask Thee to stay
Close by me forever and love me I pray.
Bless all the dear children in Thy tender care,
And take us to heaven to live with Thee there.

would take place, and parents and aunts and uncles would come to help us celebrate. As was the custom, one of the local villagers dressed up as Santa Claus and distributed the gifts we had chosen for each other. They usually consisted of soaps, little plastic guns, dolls made from mop heads, marbles, rubber balls and knick-knacks. No matter what, the gifts were always appreciated. As each gift was handed out and unwrapped, the smiles grew bigger.

Baked goodies—shortbread, fruitcake, molasses cookies— were also part of our celebration, as was the singing of carols—everyone joined in! I especially liked "Away in a Manger" and "O Holy Night." The spirit of it all lingered in the air long after we'd gathered up our belongings and made our way home through the freshly fallen snow.

"Misty-eyed, I think of home again."

Rita's Tea Room, Big Pond

This was the start of our Christmas break. I would take one last look at the spruce in all its sparkling finery, knowing that when we returned after the holidays, the tree would be gone, its decorations put away for another season and the tree itself thrown out. That always made me sad, but my father would reassure me that the discarded tree would eventually take root and come back again in all its glory.

On my way home, I would hold on tightly to the present I had received at the party. I remember getting socks one year, and another year ribbons for my hair, but the gift I remember best consisted of two beautiful glass Scottie dogs. I don't recall the name of the person who gave me such a wonderful gift—I was only about seven at the time—but as I walked along the road, the falling snow bounced off the glass and disappeared into the air, and I clutched them ever more tightly, hoping the day would never end.

Visions of Sugar Plums

bout a seven-minute walk down the road from the little schoolhouse was my father's general store, where my family lived in quarters at the back. I couldn't wait to get home after school, for we were also preparing for Christmas there. As the holiday season grew closer, the stock of Christmas goodies in the store grew and grew. Tinsel garlands and cardboard cut-outs of Santa blossomed on the walls. Alongside the usual penny candy—licorice pipes, blackballs, jelly snakes, pink bubble gum and five-cent candy bars—new treats appeared. Candy canes, foil-wrapped chocolates and brightly striped green-and-red candies filled the glass jars. Small boxes of wrapped and ribboned fudge my mother had made were also for sale. All this on the wooden counters was a tempting display for any child.

We had gas pumps out front, so my father would often leave the store to pump gas. Sometimes the travellers would come into the store, and we children always liked to take a peek and see whether we recognized them. If I didn't know them, I would note

25

My den at home, ready for the special season

their clothing, facial expressions and the kind of car they drove. I would wonder who they were and what their lives were like, and I would make up stories in my imagination about them. Around Christmas the traffic was often heavier as people set out for holiday visits, but it might stop completely when bad weather made the roads hazardous. Back then, it wasn't uncommon for the road to be closed due to a heavy snowfall.

If the adults grumbled about the storms and the inclement weather, we children delighted in the large amounts of snow that would fall. It was a simpler, more innocent time, without the distractions of television and video games—a time when snowball fights were all the rage and we were happy to keep busy building forts and snowmen. My sisters and I, along with my cousins who lived close by and other children from the village, would set up teams—each one building a fort—to see who could outlast the other. We played outside for hours, until dusk had fallen on the village and our hunger got the better of us.

We were never bored. When we weren't creating forts or snowmen, we were out in back of the store sliding down the frozen gully on large pieces of cardboard, skidding unpredictably down the bumpy surface where the water had frozen unevenly, delighting in every moment. Homemade sleighs were popular, as well as long toboggans. We took to the hills, filling the air with our laughter as we barrelled down—usually sideways—falling like rag dolls at the bottom, mittens flying, arms and legs entangled, but never too weary to climb back up and go down again.

The Christmas break brought days filled with play, during which we were outside more than we were in. The many little ponds around the village allowed us plenty of opportunities to skate. We

Cookie Cutter Ornaments

Materials

paper plates • cookie cutters (different sizes and shapes) • crayons, markers, coloured pencils, paint • glue • felt in different colours • scissors • hole punch • yarn

Instructions

1. Trace cookie cutters onto plates, and cut out.
2. Colour as desired.
3. Glue to a piece of felt, then cut the felt to match the shape of the ornament.
4. Using the hole punch, punch a hole at the top, thread yarn through the hole and tie.

Left: Christmas in my parlour, with a Victorian theme that is especially rich and colourful during the Christmas season

would weave in and out of the tall bulrushes that protruded from the glassy ponds, our feet frozen and numb from being outside too long. Still, we were having so much fun that we would forget our feet—and the time. Eventually, with hands as cold as ice, we'd untie our skates and put our boots on and head for home, our skate laces knotted together and the skates slung over our shoulders.

Kids of all ages would play pickup hockey for hours on Margaree Pond.

I knew my mother would have homemade treats waiting for us. No matter what the weather was like outside, when Mom was home warmth filled the house. Our kitchen was not very big, but Mom always had something on the go. She did her cooking and baking on an old-fashioned coal stove. She made sure it was good and hot and kept it stoked with plenty of coal. The coal scuttle was close by, ready to replenish the supply in the stove whenever it got low. There was a warming oven above the stove to keep things warm if necessary.

I would sit on my little rocker and watch my mother perform her magic with tea biscuits, apple pies with tender crusts and bannock— a dense and chewy bread that the Scots were very fond of (it's great hot from the oven with butter, or even a little molasses). The pies often bubbled over in the oven, filling the air with a delicious aroma.

We all loved it when my mother would make boiled icing. When she'd finally finished decorating whatever cake it was destined for, the rich frosting that remained in the bowl was up for grabs. I was one of eight children, and we were rarely all at home at the same time, but those of us who were there each got a spoon to clean the bowl.

My mother also made wonderful cornbread, as well as delicious molasses cookies. I used to love to watch as she poured the black-strap molasses into the bowl to make those cookies—it poured out slow and thick, in an almost stately and deliberate fashion, teasing us with its warm, heavy smell and leaving our taste buds impatient for the first bite of the rich, chewy cookies.

After she had taken the baked goods out of the oven, she would place them on the counter and open the window a shade to cool them down. We children all hung around like little birds, waiting for

The Christmas Tree

No one knows exactly when the tree began its long association with Christmas, but it probably started in Germany. By the sixteenth century, German homes at Christmas had trees hung with dolls and sugar. If they couldn't afford one, they would use a pyramid of wood in the shape of a tree and decorate it with evergreen branches.

One folk legend tells of a miraculous event on the night of Christ's birth. All the trees in the cold, snowy forests suddenly bloomed with flowers and fruit. The Christmas tree is decorated in memory of that beautiful morning of the first Noel.

"I see the mountains, feel the salt air. I have reason to believe."

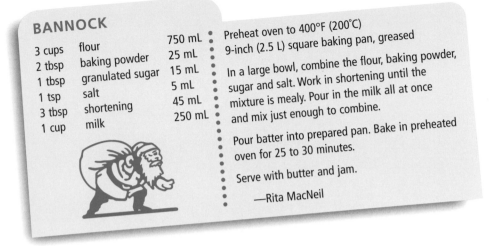

BANNOCK

3 cups	flour	750 mL
2 tbsp	baking powder	25 mL
1 tbsp	granulated sugar	15 mL
1 tsp	salt	5 mL
3 tbsp	shortening	45 mL
1 cup	milk	250 mL

Preheat oven to 400°F (200°C)
9-inch (2.5 L) square baking pan, greased

In a large bowl, combine the flour, baking powder, sugar and salt. Work in shortening until the mixture is mealy. Pour in the milk all at once and mix just enough to combine.

Pour batter into prepared pan. Bake in preheated oven for 25 to 30 minutes.

Serve with butter and jam.

—Rita MacNeil

our treats. If the window was opened high enough, it was not uncommon to later find that a pie had gone missing, taken by some local boys who couldn't resist the temptation once the smell wafted out the window.

My mother took such pride in her baking—and with good reason. She never used measuring spoons or cups. She seemed to know just the right amounts to put in, and she always said the trick to baking was to handle the dough as little as possible. Friends and family folks often dropped by—especially over the holidays—to sample her delectable baking, and they would ask for her recipes. I wish she had written them down so we could duplicate them today, but unfortunately they have disappeared over the years.

In our home, the Christmas tree was always in our living room, a room used every day. Our living quarters were very small, and the

Mother's Kitchen

Rita MacNeil

Mother if I had you back
I'd tell you what I'd do
I'd cook a Christmas dinner
Especially for you

I'd sit you at the table
And stand beside your chair
And pass you every dish
I made with tender loving care

I'd make sure you had everything
For you know I still recall
The times you were too busy
To sit for very long

You'd say you weren't that hungry
You waited on us all
I often took for granted
The effort and the love

Now once again it's Christmas
Once again I'll try
With all my kitchen gadgets
I'll ponder in my mind

How did you make it happen?
With so few pots and pans
The biscuits and the bannock
Along with homemade jams

Whatever was the magic
It was truly yours alone
You drew us to your kitchen
The heart of every home

O Christmas Tree

Traditional

O Christmas tree, O Christmas tree,
thy leaves are so unchanging.
O Christmas tree, O Christmas tree,
thy leaves are so unchanging.
Not only green when summer's here,
but also when 'tis cold and drear.
O Christmas tree, O Christmas tree,
thy leaves are so unchanging.

O Christmas tree, O Christmas tree,
you fill all hearts with gaiety.
O Christmas tree, O Christmas tree,
you fill all hearts with gaiety.
On Christmas Day you stand so tall,
affording joy to one and all.
O Christmas tree, O Christmas tree,
you fill all hearts with gaiety.

tree was picked to suit the size of our living space. Father was always the one who went to chop down the tree. Some years the tree he brought back on Christmas Eve was beautiful, while other times it fell short—meaning it was not as full as it could have been. He would place the tree in a corner, sparse side to the wall, while the fuller branches faced outward. More often than not, he'd have to rig up a support with string and anchor the tree to the wall so it wouldn't topple over.

Our parents and older siblings were in charge of decorating, while we younger children got to watch. In those days, all our ornaments were of light spun glass. The ornaments I remember were red, green and silver; some were shaped like balls, others were in the shape of bells, usually silver with red or green stripes. They reminded me of ribbon candy. A few of the ball-shaped ornaments had an old-world Santa painted on them—over time, his jolly face looked faded—and these were my favourite. All these ornaments were kept for years, and with careful handling, most stood the test of time. We also had tinsel, and a few lights strung among the branches, as well as a red-and-green garland that was wrapped around and around the deep green spruce.

When Father placed the silver star on the very top branch, we all sat back and admired our handiwork. Once the lights were turned on, I was transfixed. I could sit for hours looking at the decorations. The tree added so much colour to the room, and it was a treat to see it alight.

O Holy Night

T he church played an important role in our village. It was the centre that pulled everyone together and, like the Christmas tree, it stood as a symbol of what the season was all about. It was in that church, called St. Mary's, that the message of the birth of our Lord and all its wonderment came to life.

It was not a big church—it could hold perhaps a hundred people when it was full—but it seemed to dominate our tiny village. Covered in wood shingles, it had rows of arched windows on either side and a rather tall steeple, which housed a large, resonant bell that rang out especially joyfully on Christmas Day. The inside was all dark wood, dimly lit with candles, and at Christmastime the smell of incense filled the air. Each of the village's families had their own pew, and the more prominent or better-off folk sat at the front of the church.

The road up to the church was steep, and usually a chore to climb in the wintertime. Upon entering through the big front doors, you landed in a small foyer. To either side were small wooden staircases

The beloved St. Mary's Church in Big Pond

39

leading up to the balcony. There you would find more pews that looked down onto the parishioners below, as well as at the altar. There was also a big pipe organ upstairs. (I don't recall ever hearing it played, but it sure looked impressive.) Behind the organ was a thick rope that was used to ring the bell in the belfry that towered high above the church.

If you were ever late for church, it was no good sneaking up the stairs—the wooden stairs creaked with every step you took—but in those days the priest said mass in Latin, with his back to the congregation for the most part, so if you were lucky, you could get to your seat before he turned around.

There was a place for the holy water on either side of the aisle at the front of the church and, just before the altar, rows of red and white votive candles, which were usually lit by folks asking special favours through prayer. At the very back of the church was the confessional box where our sins were heard weekly. At Christmastime, some of the men were rather jolly when they entered the confessional:

The Poinsettia

A poor girl was going to church one Christmas Eve, and having no money to buy a present for the Christ child, she gathered some wild plants by the roadside and carried them to lay on the altar at the nativity scene. The other children laughed at her meagre gift of weeds, but the little girl insisted that she wanted to give the baby a present. When she knelt at the altar, the green leaves were miraculously transformed into the jewel-like red and white poinsettia leaves that we know today.

Others say that when the Star of Bethlehem appeared to show the world the way to the place of Christ's birth in the manger, the earth responded by creating a flower that was shaped like a star, with white petals and a golden centre. When Christ died on the cross, some of the flowers changed the colour of their petals to red as a reminder of his blood and some remained white to symbolize the purity of his sacrifice.

it wasn't uncommon to hear the clink of a flask falling accidentally to the floor.

As children, we were expected to show respect in the house of worship and were told never to speak out loud or be fidgety. It could be an over-whelming experience for little ones, but every year we all looked forward to going to midnight Mass, young and old alike. The walk to the church from the store was only about ten minutes, and we all made the walk together.

When you entered the church, you were greeted by a large wooden cross. It was at the very back of the church, behind the altar, and it seemed to take up the entire wall. On one of the side walls were the Stations of the Cross, depicting

the road to Calvary. I remember them being in large wooden frames, with images that held your attention no matter what your age. The first Station was Jesus being sentenced by Pontius Pilate, and each of the next depicted an event on the day of the Crucifixion, ending with

Jesus being taken down from the cross after his death. They were all very dramatic and sad, but since we were joyously celebrating the birth of Jesus, not his death, we didn't focus on those images on Christmas Eve.

If the inside of the church was a bit too sombre, you could pause outside at the Nativity scene set up to the right of the church, just as you came up the hill. I remember seeing a few small Nativity scenes in the houses of aunts and uncles, but the one outside the church was much bigger than any of those. The faces of the larger-than-life statues—or at least they appeared so to a child—actually seemed to come alive the closer you got. Mother Mary had a smile that reached out to everyone; Joseph, his head bowed, looked gently at the baby Jesus in the crib; and there were shepherds, as well as donkeys, angels, oxen and a baby lamb. The plaster statues seemed to capture true feeling, and in their state of grace they created a radiant contrast to the stern surroundings.

The church itself had few decorations other than the glow of candles, the smell of incense and the manger outside. The parish priest, Father Stanley, did not see the need to decorate it.

Another reason I so vividly remember midnight Mass was that the local choir, comprised of a few ladies from the village, would

break into glorious songs, lifting everyone's spirits. It was hard not to sway back and forth to their powerful refrains, usually sung in Latin, but we were always warned that the church was no place for such a display. There was one woman's voice that stood out from all the rest. A tall woman with dark hair, Hilley had such a powerful, true voice that it sent shivers through me. I was struck by each soaring note, which she seemed able to hold and carry with such ease. She added richness to the ceremony, and the emotion she poured into her singing was felt by all.

O Holy Night

Traditional

O holy night, the stars are brightly
shining;
It is the night of the dear Saviour's
birth!
Long lay the world in sin and
error pining,
Till He appeared and the soul felt
its worth.
A thrill of hope, the weary soul
rejoices,
For yonder breaks a new and
glorious morn.

Refrain
Fall on your knees, O hear the
angel voices!
O night divine, O night when
Christ was born!
O night, O holy night, O night
divine!

Led by the light of faith serenely
beaming,
With glowing hearts by His cradle
we stand.

So led by light of a star sweetly
gleaming,
Here came the wise men from
Orient land.
The King of kings lay thus in
lowly manger,
In all our trials born to be our
friend!

Refrain

Truly He taught us to love one
another;
His law is love and His Gospel is
peace.
Chains shall He break for the
slave is our brother
And in His Name all oppression
shall cease.
Sweet hymns of joy in grateful
chorus raise we,
Let all within us praise His holy
Name!

Refrain

Interior of St. Mary's Church, Big Pond

After the choir had sung some hymns, Father Stanley would enter in his colourful vestments. Father Stanley was probably in his forties when I first began to take notice of him. He seemed old to me, perhaps because he had a head of white hair and always wore black.

The First Christmas

In those days Caesar Augustus issued a decree that a census should be taken of the entire Roman world. (This was the first census that took place while Quirinius was governor of Syria.) And everyone went to his own town to register.

So Joseph also went up from the town of Nazareth in Galilee to Judea, to Bethlehem the town of David, because he belonged to the house and line of David. He went there to register with Mary, who was pledged to be married to him and was expecting a child. While they were there, the time came for the baby to be born, and she gave birth to her firstborn, a son. She wrapped him in cloths and placed him in a manger, because there was no room for them in the inn.

And there were shepherds living out in the fields nearby, keeping watch over their flocks at night. An angel of the Lord appeared to them, and the glory of the Lord shone around them, and they were terrified. But the angel said to them, "Do not be afraid. I bring you good news of great joy that will be for all the people. Today in the town of David a Saviour has been born to you; he is Christ the Lord. This will be a sign to you: You will find a baby wrapped in cloths and lying in a manger." Suddenly a great company of the heavenly host appeared with the angel, praising God and saying, "Glory to God in the highest, and on earth peace to men on whom his favour rests."

—Luke 2:1–20

When he delivered his words of wisdom during the sermon, I didn't understand much of what he was saying, especially when I was really small, but his voice commanded attention as it sounded throughout the church. The little wooden pews made squeaking sounds when people knelt down to pray, and they seemed to me the most uncomfortable apparatuses I had ever encountered. I am sure they left permanent dents on everyone's knees.

When I became bored (as surely all small children do during sermons), I would glance around me and note the hats all the women were wearing, as was the custom in church at the time—a strange

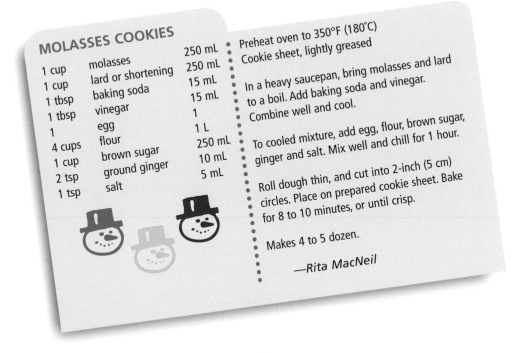

MOLASSES COOKIES

1 cup	molasses	250 mL
1 cup	lard or shortening	250 mL
1 tbsp	baking soda	15 mL
1 tbsp	vinegar	15 mL
1	egg	1
4 cups	flour	1 L
1 cup	brown sugar	250 mL
2 tsp	ground ginger	10 mL
1 tsp	salt	5 mL

Preheat oven to 350°F (180°C)
Cookie sheet, lightly greased

In a heavy saucepan, bring molasses and lard to a boil. Add baking soda and vinegar. Combine well and cool.

To cooled mixture, add egg, flour, brown sugar, ginger and salt. Mix well and chill for 1 hour.

Roll dough thin, and cut into 2-inch (5 cm) circles. Place on prepared cookie sheet. Bake for 8 to 10 minutes, or until crisp.

Makes 4 to 5 dozen.

—Rita MacNeil

array of odd head-coverings of all descriptions. Some wore scarves, while others wore knitted tams. The wealthier ladies wore black or grey felt hats with fancy hatpins in them. No matter what, girls and women were not allowed inside without a head-covering of some kind, so some girls who didn't own hats wore Kleenex fastened on by bobby pins.

When the mass was over, we left the church to the final refrain of the choir, and as they sang their last notes, the big brown doors closed behind us. We all lived fairly close to one another, friends and relatives alike, so the walk home from church was filled with good wishes for one and all. All the way home, I wondered if I would catch a glimpse of Santa and his reindeer. The night air was crisp and cold, and the moon shone brilliantly across the sky, leaving no place for him to hide, but hard as I strained my eyes, I saw nothing.

After midnight Mass, we were allowed to stay up for a half hour, enough time to have milk and one of Mom's molasses cookies (leaving the same out for Santa Claus), while the adults had a piece of rabbit pie. That was a tradition that went on for years. My father and many others shared the rabbits and the women made the pies for Christmas Eve.

Once we were in bed, the effort to stay awake soon had the opposite effect. I am sure our parents prayed we wouldn't get up too early. It was usually dark when we did rise, though, and we'd head out to the living room to see if Santa had come.

For What We Are About to Receive . . .

We were always told that if we misbehaved, Santa would leave us a lump of coal. We must have been good, because he never did. Although there were not a lot of presents under the tree, I remember the love. But most of all I remember my favourite gift of all time—a doll cradle my father made for me. It actually rocked back and forth, and inside was a tiny rag doll, one my sister had made from an old mop head. I was told the cradle was from Santa, but I learned the truth later. I also recall my sister getting a pair of red skates, and once my older brother got a pair of boxing gloves. As well, being a carpenter, my father often made wagons and sleighs.

One Christmas my father walked to town to buy our gifts. He was twelve miles from Sydney and the roads were closed, so he walked the rest of the way there and all the way back home—some twenty-four miles—with a bag on his back. He arrived home at

A typical sight around Cape Breton—the barn

twelve o'clock Christmas Eve. He was determined to do what he could to make Christmas happen for us, and he truly was Santa that year.

Another Christmas stands out: our Christmas present came by way of a new baby brother. He arrived home on December 25, and we were all very excited. The year was 1950, and he was our present, along with a bag of oranges.

My Aunt Mary, Mom's sister, would make us coats from time to time, usually out of wool fabric, or sometimes knitted sweaters and mittens. In our stockings, which were on the floor by the tree, we would find apples and oranges and a few candy kisses. In all our excitement, we sometimes forgot to see if Santa had eaten his cookies. Sure enough, he would have—or at least half of them—and he'd finish the milk as well.

Toys placed around my home at Christmastime

My Father Was a Carpenter

Rita MacNeil

Harder times brought worry lines
A furrow on your brow
You cursed the nail that went astray
But still you carried on

Christmas you say, not humbug to you
You strapped a sack upon your back
And trodded through the snow
For you became the Santa Claus
That we would come to know

A simple task I think not!
Your shoulders carried all
With little hungry mouths to feed
Christmastime and all

And what of gifts and what of mirth
You knew the story well
The forest held the perfect tree
The one that you would fell

And what of wishes in the night
While gazing at the stars
Little voices crying out
"Santa here we are!"

You knew the task before you
You handled it quite well
All the things you made from wood
You did with loving care

So once again it's Christmas
Your memory I recall
Your hands were always busy
With the hammer and the saw

Mistletoe

The word *mistletoe* is said to come from the words *tan*, a twig, and *mistl*, different, because it is different from the trees it twines around and lives on. The Roman author Pliny described the use of mistletoe by the British Druids. He wrote that they honoured the plant both because it stayed strong and green throughout the winter, and for its medicinal powers. They believed it was a cure for sterility and a remedy against poison.

In Brittany, mistletoe is called *herbe de las croix*, or *lignum crucis*. According to the story, it was once a tall, straight tree, and the cross on which Jesus was crucified was made of its wood. After that, it was punished by being transformed into a parasitic evergreen that must depend on other trees for its life. A version of this story is also told in Norse myth. The summer sun god, Balder, was killed by the blind winter god, Hoder, with an arrow made of the wood of the mistletoe. Balder's mother prayed for her child to be restored to life, and when her wish was granted, the mistletoe was changed into a charm against danger, and everyone who passed under a bough of mistletoe received a kiss for good luck.

And why is mistletoe hung in doorways? Because it was used by the Druids as part of a winter solstice ritual. Five days following the first full moon after the winter solstice, the Druids gave boughs of mistletoe to the people to decorate their doors, where its powers of protection kept evil spirits from entering the houses.

Now that we were all up and busy with our gifts, my mother would turn her attention to the Christmas dinner, which was always at noon. The meal consisted of turkey and stuffing, carrots, turnips and potatoes. Usually, the vegetables came from my grandmother's farm, which was just up the hill behind the store. Mom's cooking was simple but always very good. Her potatoes were cooked and mashed with a bit of cream. The carrots were left whole, cooked and then sprinkled with white pepper and butter. For her stuffing she used stale bread crumbs, onions, savory, sage, an egg, salt and pepper, and sometimes the turkey giblets, which had been cooked and finely chopped. Her gravy was the best I have ever tasted. She would brown the onions first, then add flour and water to the pan, and

WILD RICE AND ORANGE STUFFING

2 tbsp	butter	25 mL
1/2 cup	chopped celery	125 mL
1/4 cup	chopped onion	50 mL
1/4 tsp	Tabasco	1 mL
1 cup	uncooked wild rice	250 mL
3-1/2 cups	toasted bread cubes	825 mL
2 tsp	orange rind	10 mL
2 tsp	salt	10 mL
1 tsp	poultry seasoning	5 mL
1/2 tsp	rosemary	2 mL
6	oranges	6

Melt butter in a skillet. Add celery and onion and cook until soft, but not brown. Stir in Tabasco.

Prepare and cook wild rice according to package directions.

Combine celery, onion, wild rice, bread cubes, orange rind, salt, poultry seasoning and rosemary.

To section oranges, slice from top and bottom; cut off peel, removing any white membrane. Cut each orange segment in half. Add to wild rice mixture. Toss lightly.

Makes 7 cups (1.75 L).

—Rita MacNeil

when the thick gravy was poured, there wasn't a lump to be found. All her touches were her own creations and her little secrets, and I've always felt over the years that she made the best-tasting food ever.

We all sat at the kitchen table, and before the meal, we gave thanks. I don't recall dinner guests—only the immediate family

Mummers

Belsnickles in Virginia, Hogmanay guisers in Scotland, and janneys and mummers in Newfoundland are all examples of an old custom that shows up in late-winter holiday traditions throughout Europe, and goes back to ancient times. Ever since the Roman Saturnalia and the medieval Lord of Misrule, there has been a tradition of revellers disguising themselves, acting silly and turning logic upside down. In Newfoundland the custom is called "mummering." People cover their faces with masks, disguise their bodies with layers of quilts and sheets and old clothes, and alter their voices by speaking on indrawn breaths. Men often dress up as women, known as *oonshooks* or *owenchuks*. The name comes from an Irish word, *oonshugh*, meaning "a foolish woman." The object of the game is to be unrecognizable to people who have known you all your life.

Once they are in costume, the mummers walk to their neighbours' houses, knock and call out, "Any mummers allowed in?" If they are told no, they go away at once. If they are invited in, they will continue their outlandish behaviour, sometimes dancing, sometimes refusing to speak, while their hosts try to guess their identities. They will be offered food and drink, but they often refuse. If the male mummers accept a drink of rum, they must take off their masks. Little mummers (children) are given cake or sweets.

The first Noel

Traditional

The first Noel, the angels did say,
Was to certain poor shepherds in fields as they lay;
In fields where they lay keeping their sheep,
On a cold winter's night that was so deep.

Chorus
Noel, Noel, Noel, Noel,
Born is the King of Israel.

They looked up and saw a star,
Shining in the East beyond them far;
And to the earth it gave great light,
And so it continued day and night.

Chorus

This star drew nigh to the northwest;
O'er Bethlehem it took its rest,
And there it did both stop and stay,
Right o'er the place where Jesus lay.

Chorus

members—but I do remember that my mother didn't sit down with us. She served the meal and ate a little after we were all done. From what I have learned over the years, this custom of the mother serving the family and tending to herself later was common in many households.

After Christmas dinner, I usually went outside to play with my cousins, who lived close by. Neighbours not too far away had children our age, and two of my sisters would sometimes join us. We would be excited to play in the snow and talk about the gifts Santa had brought. We could look up and see the smoke coming from the chimneys of the homes nearby, and I often wondered how those inside spent their Christmases. Though we never really heard any stories, I am sure hardships were plentiful back then.

By the time bedtime came around, with a full day of play and full tummies, we children were all more than ready for sleep. We'd go to our bedrooms, where the windows would sometimes be coated with a thin film of ice, left by Jack Frost. When I gently blew on the glass, images appeared. The tall castles or feathery plumes or the half-hidden faces of elves and fairies filled my imagination as I drifted off to dreamland.

Have Yourself a Merry Little . . .

When I left my childhood behind and was married with children of my own, I tried to recreate the old-time Christmases I remembered from my childhood. No matter where I was living, I was always up for the challenge. I worked on creating a warm and colourful atmosphere. Imagination was the key, and I placed anything and everything that spoke to the child in me throughout the rooms where we would be celebrating.

If I didn't have a tablecloth, I could make do with a large white bedsheet, to which I sewed lots of red and green ribbons. For a centrepiece, I sprayed acorns with hairspray—which made them last longer and also made them shiny—and put them in a glass bowl on top of red and green tissue paper. I tied ribbon around the cutlery to give it a new look. Little touches like these made for a fine-looking table. I also enjoyed placing little toy figurines all around the table—angels, toy soldiers and whatever else I could find at stores like Bargain Harold's or Woolworth's.

Rita's dining-room table, set for Christmas dinner

I tried to find Christmas ornaments for my tree that were like the ones I had seen at home as a child. I still prefer the more traditional ornaments. I have collected silver-coloured glass balls with Santa painted on, just like the ones I loved back then. They are still my favourite ones.

I made use of the Christmas cards that came in the mail, stringing them above the doorways. The scenes on the cards were always so

eye-catching. Whether they
were of a religious nature, or
depicted a big red Santa high
in the sky in a red sleigh with
reindeer, or simply captured
the beauty of the falling snow,
they all celebrated the joy of
Christmas. I hung wreaths from
my door and my windows,
and I loved the look of a single
candle burning in each window.

Opening the gifts was
always saved for Christmas
morning. My husband, David,
and I would hide all the
presents away and then,
when our children had gone to
bed on Christmas Eve—having
put out milk and cookies for
Santa—we would take great
pleasure in looking at the gifts again before we wrapped them all. As
Wade and Laura snuggled up in their beds, we would read them "The
Night Before Christmas," knowing full well they would be awake for
hours, listening for Santa Claus.

They would be up around five in the morning and would come
to wake us, their excitement bubbling over. Once we were all downstairs, we'd turn on the lights on the tree and put some Christmas
music on in the background. David and I would watch in delight as

our children's eyes grew bigger with each gift they opened. There they sat by the tree they'd helped decorate, surrounded by boxes and brightly coloured papers, happily lost in their own world. We also hung stockings up for them, and David took great pride in stuffing them until they overflowed. Every little present he put in them he wrapped individually—it took them longer to go through

Christmas Playdough

Materials

1 cup	flour	250 mL
1/2 cup	salt	125 mL
2 tsp	cream of tartar	10 mL
2 tbsp	vegetable oil	25 mL
1 cup	water	250 mL

green and red food colouring

Instructions

1. In a large bowl, mix the flour and salt and stir well.

2. Add cream of tartar and mix.

3. Add vegetable oil and mix.

4. Add water slowly while mixing steadily.

5. Put half the dough into a medium bowl.

6. Add a few drops of green food colouring to one mixture and a few drops of red food colouring to the other and stir. Continue to add food colouring until the dough has reached the desired shade.

7. Put each mixture into a saucepan and stir over medium heat until pliable.

When finished playing, store any excess play dough in an airtight container in the refrigerator.

Christmas Gift-Giving

The Christmas tradition of gift-giving was begun in the fourth century AD by Nicholas, the archbishop of Myra, a seaport town in Asia Minor. As a young man, Nicholas had inherited great wealth on the death of his parents. He wanted to give his money away to people who needed and deserved help, but he wanted to do it modestly, so people wouldn't know the source of the gift.

A poor man in the town feared his three daughters would die unmarried because he had no money for their dowries. Hearing of this, Nicholas passed by his house at night and tossed a bag of gold in through the window. His scheme was successful and the first daughter's wedding celebration was soon held. Encouraged, Nicholas went back with a bag of gold for the second daughter, and again a marriage was the happy result. But when he returned the third time, the grateful father was watching and knelt before the shy priest, thanking him and asking why he hid his good deeds. Nicholas would not consent to have his kindness made public and asked the father to tell no one . . . but the truth eventually came to be known and the legend of Saint Nicholas was born.

their stockings than it did to open all the other gifts! For myself, I couldn't ask for a greater gift than my two children, who always showed love and appreciation for everything they received.

Once all the hoopla was over and each gift had been opened—which usually took a few hours—David would play with the children, assembling certain gifts and making them ready for use. With the sound of their laughter in the background, I would get

Rita's children, Laura and Wade, with Rita's niece Julie between them

Rita's son, Wade

Wade and Laura next to their grandmother, Lillian

dinner ready. Like my mother, I started early and kept the dishes simple. Of course, I added things like broccoli, Brussels sprouts and cauliflower—vegetables I hadn't heard of until I was older. No matter how I tried, the dinner never tasted quite like my mother's, but we all enjoyed it just the same.

Later in the day, friends would drop by, and we would go visiting and meet up with other friends and relatives, sharing pleasantries about our day and expressing our wishes for peace and joy for the days ahead.

After I became a divorced parent, things changed, but together or separate, David and I have always made sure Christmas was special for Wade and Laura. He has spent Christmas Day with us for as long as I can remember, and he still fills the stockings to the brim. We now have four beautiful grandchildren—Aden, Rachel, Anthony and Zoe—and so the circle continues.

70

Anthony, Aden and Rachel with Rita

Christmas at Home

No matter where I have lived over the years, I have kept Christmas in the old traditional way. Even though I am now able to buy that special tablecloth or Christmas dish, not a whole lot has changed. It's still the usual scurrying around, shopping, getting that special present, decorating now not one but two trees.

In my home in Sydney, I have a lovely parlour that is furnished in Victorian style with pieces I have collected over the years, as well as some reproductions. At Christmastime the parlour comes alive with candlelight. The trees themselves are decorated with a Victorian theme. In the course of my touring, I have purchased many different Christmas ornaments. I like the German-made glass ornaments shaped like little churches, red with gold trim, because they have that old-fashioned look to them, and I love the lights that look like white candles when they're placed on the branches. The tops for my trees are angels that light up and give off a soft glow.

Up my staircase I have wooden toy soldiers in an array of colours. They stand two feet tall, and the ones on either side of my two fireplaces stand three feet tall. They add a childlike atmosphere to the house. Painted trays and sleighs depicting vivid scenes in rich, dark colours adorn certain alcoves and corners throughout the downstairs of my home. Everywhere you look, there is some small reminder of Christmas.

Then there are the many festive dishes I have collected, sporting a sprig of holly or a toy soldier or children playing in the snow. These are the things that catch my eye when I go into the Christmas stores while I'm on tour. (One of my favourite stores is The Spirit of

Victorian Potpourri Ornaments

Materials

round clear glass ornaments
loose potpourri
dried miniature rosebuds
glue gun

Instructions

1. Carefully remove the metal top of the ornament.

2. Push the potpourri into the ornament until full and replace the top of the ornament.

3. Cut the rosebuds off their stems. Using the glue gun, glue the buds in a circle around the top of the ornament.

Christmas in Victoria, B.C.) When I set my holiday table now, I am able to display all these lovely pieces—and I keep them in a hutch in my dining room, so I get to see them year-round.

Along with my children and grandchildren, David and his partner, Paula, come for dinner each year, and I do the cooking with pleasure.

Christmas at Home

Music and Lyrics by Rita MacNeil

Memories of walking home
From the Christmas party in the
    falling snow
Exchanging gifts, exchanging
    smiles
Hanging pine cones in the hall

Chorus
Merry Christmas meant lots of
    whispering
Special feelings to bridge the
    difference
All the years we came together
For Christmas at home

And the radio played in the
    distance
O Night, O Holy Night

Memories of old Jack Frost
Frozen pictures upon the glass
Changing right before your eyes
With a warm breath from the
    happy child

Chorus

Memories of walking home
From the Christmas party in the
    falling snow
Exchanging gifts, exchanging
    smiles
Hanging pine cones in the hall

Chorus

And the radio played in the
    distance
O Night, O Holy Night

I have learned a few tricks to make the work easier. I set my table on Christmas Eve, and I spend a great deal of time fussing over each detail, to make sure everything will run smoothly when I'm preparing the meal. I try to take everyone's particular likes into consideration. Besides the traditional turkey with all the trimmings, I usually cook salmon or halibut for those who prefer fish to fowl.

Cooking some of the vegetables—like turnips, carrots and mashed potatoes— a day ahead makes things much simpler and cuts down on the pots and pans I have to deal with on Christmas Day. I also cook the turkey on Christmas Eve so I can freeze the drippings and remove the

layer of fat that forms on the top. Now I only buy and cook the turkey breast—I find there is less waste. I make my stuffing using mashed potatoes, onions, bread crumbs, celery salt and pepper. I take pride in my gravy, which usually turns out rather well.

I serve the food on the kitchen table, buffet style, and that leaves room on the dining-room table for decorations and candles. I set the kitchen table with a red and white tablecloth and candles in the shape of Santa Claus. Among the serving dishes, I place sprigs of greenery and Christmas ornaments. The dining-room table is set with a white tablecloth and red candle holders. The Christmas napkins are placed in gold napkin rings adorned with little angels playing horns. I also place little figurines among the table settings, just as I did when Wade and Laura were children. Now it's my grandchildren who get to enjoy the whimsical figurines.

The Yule Log

A cheerful Yule log, burning brightly in a hearth, is part of the bright lights of the Christmas season, along with its candles and Christmas tree lights. The desire for light during the darkest time of year has been a human wish for thousands of years. The Yule log came from a day of celebration held by the ancient Britons and Scandinavians. The day was called Yule, or Jol (which developed into the word *jolly*), and it was celebrated with a holiday fire built on a huge log that had to be big enough to burn all night. This way, they believed, the earth would be protected from eternal winter. Magic powers were known to come from the ashes of the Yule log, for one, a sprinkling of Yule ashes kept a house safe from lightening. Now, we do not believe the Yule log is magic, but it is still a beautiful and treasured part of Christmas celebrations.

80

When the ten of us are seated around the table, the grandchildren bring us all great joy with their sudden bursts of energy. My older grandson, Aden, likes to tell riddles and comes up with a new one about every ten minutes. He and his sister, Rachel, tease each other and keep the conversation alive and interesting.

Rachel has a tea trolley I keep at my house just for her, and when dinner is over and everyone is ready for a cup of tea, she has to have her little pot filled as well. All of my grandchildren love to explore in my house. I have a front stairway and a back stairway that enters into my kitchen. I also have an attic, and they are anxious to know what's up there. It's really for storage, but they like to go up and have a look anyway. Believe me, there are lots of places in my big old house to grab the attention of all three grandchildren.

I now send the gifts I buy for them over to their own houses on Christmas Eve so they can open them in the morning. It makes it less confusing, and they get to see their presents all at once. These days, I find the simpler you can keep the season, the better.

On Christmas Day, when I get the chance to sit back and watch my children with their children, I know they will be making their own Christmas traditions in the years ahead. Maybe they'll watch favourite Christmas stories like *A Christmas Carol* with Alistair Sim or Ol' Seuss's *How the Grinch Stole Christmas!* The word "compassion" comes to mind when I think of these movies. They suggest that people have the ability to change, and to bring kindness and happiness to others.

That is certainly what I wish for my children and grandchildren. May they have the strength to fulfill their dreams, whatever those dreams may be, and the wisdom to make decisions that will enrich

Aden on Santa's lap

Anthony

Laura and Rachel

Anthony

Anthony during the Christmas Season

Aden and Rachel on Santa's lap

Aden and Rachel

Anthony

Rita and Anthony

Aden and Rachel, with a new toy

A Christmas Carol

"A merry Christmas, Bob!" said Scrooge, with an earnestness that could not be mistaken, as he clapped him on the back. "A merrier Christmas, Bob, my good fellow, than I have given you for many a year! I'll raise your salary, and endeavour to assist your struggling family, and we will discuss your affairs this very afternoon, over a Christmas bowl of smoking bishop, Bob! Make up the fires, and buy another coal-scuttle before you dot another i, Bob Cratchit."

Scrooge was better than his word. He did it all, and infinitely more; and to Tiny Tim, who did not die, he was a second father. He became as good a friend, as good a master, and as good a man, as the good old city knew, or any other good old city, town, or borough, in the good old world. Some people laughed to see the alteration in him, but he let them laugh, and little heeded them; for he was wise enough to know that nothing ever happened on this globe, for good, at which some people did not have their fill of laughter in the outset; and knowing that such as these would be blind anyway, he thought it quite as well that they should wrinkle up their eyes in grins, as have the malady in less attractive forms. His own heart laughed: and that was quite enough for him.

He had no further intercourse with Spirits, but lived upon the Total Abstinence Principle, ever afterwards; and it was always said of him, that he knew how to keep Christmas well, if any man alive possessed the knowledge. May that be truly said of us, and all of us! And so, as Tiny Tim observed, God Bless Us, Every One!

—*Charles Dickens*

their lives at work and at home. Now that my son and daughter are parents, I want them to experience lasting happiness with themselves and their partners, and the endless joy their children will bring them over the years. May my four grandchildren always know how lucky they are to have such fine parents. May they have the ability to deal with this not-so-perfect world, and have as few heartaches as possible along the way. May they discover the joys that family and friends can bring and have the courage to go forward and discover their hidden talents. But for now, may they just enjoy being young, happy and healthy as they celebrate the joys of Christmas.

My favourite photo of my beautiful grandchildren

Across the Miles

It was just a matter of time, I guess, before I started to express my love for the holiday season through song. I wrote my first Christmas song, "Christmas at Home," in the eighties. The words in the song summed up memories from childhood in a couple of verses. One memory stood out in particular. My father was working on a carpentry job a fair distance from Big Pond. He wouldn't be home until late on December 24, and I got to spend the evening cuddled next to my mother while a choir sang "O Holy Night" on the old brown radio. This memory was the key to that first song of mine.

For some reason, I wrote the rest of my Christmas songs while I was touring Australia in the early nineties. I remember looking at the beautiful blue-green water and imagining it was snow—a bit of a stretch, but it worked! The church, the school, the choir, my parents and my children all played a part in the inspiration behind the songs. When my children were young, David's excitement would be equal to mine as we got ready for the big day. Even after we drifted apart,

Singing a song in my Victorian Christmas special

This Season Will Never Grow Old

Rita MacNeil

Christmas is coming, I can tell by the
smiles
I remember the snowflakes that fell from
the sky
And covered the village that lay sleeping
below
Thank goodness this season will never
grow old

I look through my window well into the
night
Watching and waiting and hoping I
might
See one little reindeer fly through the
snow
Thank goodness the season will never
grow old

Christmas is coming, may joy fill your
home
And the spirit be with you wherever
you go

Trees with full branches were the first
ones to go
I remember the children who came to
the door
And sang out the carols we all used to
know
Thank goodness this season will never
grow old

All round the fire, the warmth of the
flame
Tip-toeing softly trying not to
awake
The ones who lay waiting for good
things you know
Thank goodness this season will never
grow old

Christmas is coming, may joy fill your
home
And the spirit be with you wherever
you go

The chapel in Louisbourg—me and the Barra MacNeils

I never forgot those times, and thinking about the children and David, years later I wrote "Across the Miles Tonight."

I have been very fortunate over the years to have been able to write and record Christmas music. It has allowed me to tour the country with my Christmas shows. The tours run from the middle of November to the middle of December, and we always get home in

Once upon a Christmas
(Across the Miles Tonight)

Rita MacNeil

The apples in December were still upon
the tree
A lone bird was singing sweet by the
frozen stream
Once upon a Christmas how I long to
see
A hint of white, all is bright
You waiting for me

The ribbons and the presents were
never very far
You always knew just what to give to
touch somebody's heart
Once upon a Christmas, how it used to
be
A winter's night, all is bright
And you waiting for me

I know it's that time again, you must
feel it too
We live in different places now, it's
Christmas without you
But if I take a moment, I close my eyes
real tight

I'll send you my best wishes, across the
miles tonight

Do you watch the snowflakes fall, like
you used to do
And worry when that day arrives, forget
a gift or two
Once upon a Christmas when there was
you and me
Making lists, wrapping gifts and sharing
all our dreams

I know it's that time again, you must
feel it too
We live in different places now, it's
Christmas without you
But if I take a moment, I close my eyes
real tight
I'll send you my best wishes across the
miles tonight
I'll send you my best wishes across the
miles tonight

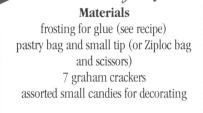

Miniature Gingerbread House

Materials		**Frosting**	
frosting for glue (see recipe)	8 oz	confectioner's (icing) sugar	250 g
pastry bag and small tip (or Ziploc bag and scissors)	3 tbsp	butter/margarine	45 mL
7 graham crackers	1/2 tsp	vanilla	2 mL
assorted small candies for decorating	1-1/2 to 2 tbsp	milk	22 to 25 mL

Instructions

1. Prepare the frosting: Mix all the ingredients together until smooth and easy to spread, but not runny. If it's too runny, add more sugar.

2. Place frosting in pastry bag and use a small tip (or use a Ziploc bag, with a small hole cut in the corner).

3. Place one graham cracker flat on the table and squeeze a little frosting in a line around all the edges.

4. Place one cracker on each side, standing up. It now looks like a box without a top. Carefully squeeze more frosting on all outside corners from top to bottom, and around the bottom of the box. Let stand for a while to let frosting harden a little. This will make working with the roof easier.

5. Squeeze frosting on two opposite top edges of the box and place the last two graham crackers in a V shape as the roof. Squeeze frosting along the top of the roof, where the crackers join. Let stand again until frosting hardens.

6. With the leftover frosting, cover the roof to look like snow. Decorate the house with candy, using a small amount of frosting as glue.

time for Christmas in Cape Breton. My last few Christmas tours have included the wonderful coal mining choir The Men of the Deeps, and when we are on the bus going from place to place, it really is like one happy family on the road.

The cities and towns we pass through are aglow with sparkly lights, colourful wreaths and other glittering decorations that brighten up the windows and doors of homes and shops. The theatres we play in usually have the foyers done up with brightly lit trees, creating a warm atmosphere for the audience when they arrive. Sharing the music night after night is like being part of a Christmas card we are sending to the audience, and when we greet folks after the show, you can feel the warmth and goodwill emanating from one person to another.

The phone calls back home are plentiful, since everyone on tour is anxious to be with their families. As the tour comes to an end, we are often nervous that flights will be delayed and the weather will hinder our travel plans. There have been some touch-and-go situations, and certainly times when a delay of a day or two has threatened our arrival time. Once, when we travelled home from out west, we made it all the way to Halifax, only to be told the pilot felt the fog was too bad to fly to Sydney. Our hearts sank. We all had family waiting for us—they'd be so disappointed. The pilot decided to go, but when we arrived over Sydney, the plane was unable to land. So back to Halifax we went, feeling deflated. The next day it was a scramble, as there were so many folk trying to get home for Christmas, but we made it. It was December 22, and once the runway at Sydney airport was in sight, we all breathed a sigh of relief and thanked the Lord for our safe return.

Spending Christmas at home is a big plus for me. I remember a special treat a few Christmases ago, when my two children hosted the celebration. First my son, Wade, and his wife, Lori, had me over on Christmas Eve. They were living in temporary quarters at the time, an old farmhouse in Big Pond I had purchased years before and have since sold. The two-storey house is simply charming. It's set back off the road, and the driveway is lined on one side with a rose-covered hedge. Driving out to Big Pond from Sydney, I watched the snow falling ever so lightly, just enough to create that perfect winter setting. When I arrived at the farmhouse, I could see soft lights glowing from inside the house, and the hedge, once filled with wild roses, was now blanketed in white. The whole scene took me back to years ago when I was a child in Big Pond.

When I finally stood on the porch and opened the front door, I was taken with how beautiful everything was. Flickering candles cast warm shadows throughout the house. The kitchen, larger than all the other rooms, had clearly been used years ago as the centre where all the family activities took place. A stairway leading up to a back bedroom was cleverly built into the kitchen. Lori and Wade had a lovely table laid out with a colourful set of Christmas dishes. What a surprise I got when I discovered they were disposable paper plates! As they prepared the meal, I glanced around and was reminded that this house had originally belonged to the McLelland family—it had been their home for years. I couldn't help but wonder how they'd spent Christmas here.

My mantel at home—"choirs of angels singing on high"

After our supper—a traditional meal of turkey and all the trimmings—we went into a smaller room, where a beautiful tree stood in the corner. They had decorated it with some of my old ornaments from years ago—some of which I'd had when Wade and Laura were little, such as the little red-and-green cloth elves I had bought at Eaton's. To see them hanging on their tree brought back such good memories. The entire evening was one I shall always treasure, for the effort that was put into the night was evident.

My daughter, Laura, and her husband, Dana, had invited me to their home for dinner the next day. And that was indeed a treat for me. I usually have them over for the Christmas meal, but this time it was my turn to sit back and enjoy. The neighbourhood, which is within the city limits of Sydney, is one where there is no shortage of decorations, each house reflecting the joy of the season. Laura's home was beautifully decorated with a tree and ornaments of various colours. There were plenty of candles, and miniature lights peeped through ivy vines on the top of her kitchen cupboards. The children were busy showing me all their toys, and when we were ready for dinner, I smiled to myself and thought how nice it was to sit down to such a wonderfully cooked meal made by my daughter. I even think she outdid me with the gravy. It was an occasion I shall never forget. Both my children had given me a Christmas to remember.

I certainly know the importance of family at Christmastime, but the friends I have made over the years also come to mind during this season. My dear friends Margaret and Gary, who live in Australia, tell me how different their Christmas is. In Brisbane, December is summertime. They enjoy barbecuing legs of pork and preparing smoked ham, chicken, roast potatoes, green salads, seafood salads

and coleslaw, along with fresh pineapple, watermelon, apricots and cherries. Plum pudding and custard are the traditional desserts. Decked out in shorts, they have dinner and dessert on their patio, where a "soaker" hose sprays fine jets of water high into the air from holes placed randomly along its length. This is put on the roof of the deck to keep it cool in the hot sun, and the yard is also full of sprinklers. Everyone keeps as cool as they can, given that the temperature is usually about forty degrees Celsius. Like us, though, they have a tree with lights and gifts underneath, to be opened on Christmas morning.

I get lots of cards from folks all over the world extending their warm wishes to me. A few young people I have met, such as Everett, Jennifer, Adrian, Amber and Judy, have sent me cards they have made, or poems, along with Christmas gifts. All these children face challenges every day due to their disabilities, but just spending a few precious moments in their presence has taught me so much about compassion.

May the world as we know it continue to rise above troubled times, and may Christmas always be a season of hope and caring.

A Gift of Love

When the time came to do my first Christmas special for television in 1990, the obvious choice of location was Cape Breton. We filmed in two locations, St. Mary's church in Big Pond and the Gowrie House in North Sydney.

A two-storey wooden mansion on Shore Road overlooking the harbour, the Gowrie House was built in 1834 by Samuel Archibald and sports two huge chimneys, two marble fireplaces and a big bay window overlooking the spacious grounds. These days, this country estate is a four-star inn that boasts the finest food and is constantly busy.

It was the perfect location. The setting was beautiful. A wide driveway of crushed stone lined by majestic trees was ideal for the horses and wagon. The wagon had seats situated so we could face each other and was pulled by two grey workhorses in black harness. The inside of Gowrie House was picture-perfect, warm and inviting. The large dining room created a place for ongoing activities, and the sweet sounds of fiddle music could be heard from the Victorian living room. The music was, of course, for the special—all part of the process of creating down-home memories.

The Barra MacNeils, with their distinct sound and clear harmonies, are truly fine musicians and singers. I was thrilled when they agreed to be part of my special.

Always entertaining, on- and off-camera, John McDermott reflects on the season in his songs and stories. His wonderful mellow voice is loved by many, and makes for memorable moments.

Patti LaBelle's rendition of "O Holy Night" rings through the church, leaving us all breathless. As her final notes soar upwards, we are reminded of what soul really means.

The delightful Natalie MacMaster keeps us mesmerized with her brilliant command of the fiddle.

Doing a Christmas special is a joy because it involves so many wonderful people. I am not the only one who gets caught up in the Christmas spirit—most of my musical guests do, too. The production crew works long hours to make us all look good and ensure the best show possible. I owe the success of my specials to all these people, and I thank the many folks who allow us into their homes to celebrate this season I so dearly love.

The memories of each special will remain with me always.

Even with a few obstacles, we all had such fun. I recall one time when the weather would not cooperate and we needed falling snow, so it was flown into Sydney airport in the form of foam and a load of potato flakes. The magic of television!

Then we moved on to film at St. Mary's church, which was lovely for me, as it was such an inspirational part of my life. When I first arrived at the church, it was by horse and wagon—how exciting! —

the same horses we'd used at the Gowrie House and the grey wooden wagon. We were shooting a night scene, and as we drove up the steep hill that led to the church, I could see the whole front of the structure framed in white lights all the way up to the tall steeple—it looked so beautiful. Stepping inside, I saw that this little country church, with its plain interior that had seemed so dark when I was a child, had come alive inside thanks to the bouquets of flowers and candles that filled the room.

Singing in the church brought my childhood memories alive. Standing at the foot of the altar, I was able to look up into the loft and imagine that choir from long ago, with Hilley's voice leading all the rest. Here, in this holy place that has seen so many village folk come and

Holly and Ivy

For ancient peoples, the holly—like other evergreens (bay, box, yew, juniper, pine, fir and spruce, to name a few)—was revered as a symbol of life because it did not lose its leaves or its fresh green colour in winter. Evergreens were used as charms to ward off devils and ghosts that came to earth along with the dark and cold of winter. The religious observances of the druids—elders, or priests, of the Britons—were associated with the oak, which symbolized strength, and the holly, representing eternal life. Ivy was also associated with life and strength. The holly and ivy together were believed to be a force protecting the people from evil. The holly's thorns were sharp, to catch and hold bad spirits, and the smoke of burning juniper twigs was used to chase demons and bad luck out of houses and stables.

107

When It Comes to Christmas

Music and Lyrics by Rita MacNeil

Did you make the Christmas cards many
years ago
And when you painted on the scene,
how did the story go
Was it bright red and green with a hint
of silver thaw
Were there happy faces behind every
door

Did you always feel somehow that you
had to show
Shoppers with their presents and the
whitest of snow
Did they rush to and fro with a special
season glow
That seems to be repeating in everyone
you know

And when it comes to Christmas
And Christmas cards we write
The meaning is no different
Peace, hope and love

Did you show that beaten path, foot-
prints in the snow
The little church upon the hill where
everybody goes
And the star shining bright and the
brightest star of all
Wherever people gather, they sing and
praise tonight

And when it comes to Christmas
And Christmas cards we write
The meaning is no different
Peace, hope and love
The meaning is no different
Peace, hope and love

Victorian village (Riverdale Farm)

go, and so many changes over the years, I felt deeply connected through the music.

I was even able to record my Christmas album inside the church, which pleased me, as I wanted the music I wrote to reflect as much as possible my childhood memories of this special place. Each song I wrote for that album had snippets of memories woven into verses, and as I sang those songs in St. Mary's, those images came to life for me.

A second special followed, and once again the songs I had written were incorporated into an hour-long television show. This time the elements of home and my memory of my grandmother came into play. We hired a grandmother figure, Emily Butler from Sydney, and even though she was a bit young to play the part, we all loved her, for she won the hearts of everyone on

Emily Butler with Rita—"good friends light a candle"

the set with her great humour and endless energy.

Emily's quiet grace reminded me of my grandmother—Mary Catherine Campbell—who had fourteen children, four of whom died in infancy. She was a strong, caring woman who knew how to drive a plough, as well as knit and look after her family.

I remember the times I went to visit her. She was always sitting in her rocker, looking out the window that faced the road leading up to her farmhouse. She was a tiny woman, slightly bent over from years of hard work. Her hair was grey and tied back into a bun, and she always wore a cotton dress with a sweater over top. In one of my songs about my grandmother, I summed up my memories of her in these words:

Two porcelain dolls in my parlour—a great conversation piece

Grandmother sat by her window
And stared out at December
Falling flakes reminded her of
The good times she once had
Some say she stared through madness
Some said it was sadness
She would gaze upon the snow
And see the blossoms there below

Her house was sparsely decorated at Christmastime, but she always had biscuits and sugar cookies ready for us children. The times we talked, I had the sense she was a woman of great dignity.

My memories always play a large part in my Christmas specials, though the music is the key. The little village of Big Pond and its surroundings, as well as the people, gave me the inspiration for the specials and will be treasured memories for years to come.

Copyright Acknowledgements